Dr. Erika M. Gibson

Dr. Erika M. Gibson
Put On Your Full Armor of God and Let's Win
The War Together!!

Publisher

Liz**C**ari **P**ublishing **I**nternational
lizcaripublishing@gmail.com

Visit the author's website at www. drerikagibson.org

Preparing Girls for War
Copyright-2017 by Dr. Erika Gibson
First Edition, 2017
Published in the United States

ISBN-978-0-9986634-0-1
ISBN-978-0-9986634-1-8 (e-book)

For information regarding special discounts for bulk purchases or to book Dr. Erika Gibson to speak at your next event, please contact drgibsonmddc@gmail.com or Preparinggirls4war.com

Names and identifying characters of certain individuals in this book have been changed in order to protect their privacy.

"The greatest victory is that which requires no battle."
— Sun Tzu, The Art of War

Table of Contents

CHAPTER 5

Preparing Girls

For

War

Dr. Erika M. Gibson

Publisher

LizCari Publishing International
lizcaripublishing@gmail.com

Dedication

Dedication

This book is dedicated to all young women who are committed to winning the war!

A special dedication to my daughter,

Hailey Elizabeth Gibson,

who will inevitably face the many trials and tribulations of life!

My prayer is that each of you will carry the shield of protection with you as you travel through life's challenging journey.

The content of the book is not to judge your lifestyle, but to provide guidance in making good sound decisions.

Acknowledgments

Acknowledgments

A special thanks to Dr. Clayton Gibson, III, my husband, supporter and contributing author who continues to motivate me to follow my dreams and to live within my divine purpose.

Thanks to my children Hailey and Haiden for allowing me to snip their time in order to make my dream a reality.

A special thanks to my parents, Cary and Maggie for giving me the tools to Fight the War and Win!

Thanks to WordSharp.net my editor for their expertise and expedient responses.

Kudos to my friend, classmate and reviewer Valour Taylor Cobbins, who graciously wrote the Foreword for this piece of work and for reviewing my first draft.

Thanks to Bateen Studio for the wonderful Book Cover Design

A special thanks to Dr. George Tucker (Ob/Gyn) for allowing me to see first-hand how our teens are fighting daily to win the war!

Thanks to a great group of people who gave of their time to review my work and provide feed-back:

Dr. Tricia Moss – Atlanta Pediatrician
Mrs. Paula Finley – Healthcare Executive

Foreword

Foreword

by Valour Taylor Cobbins

I first met Erika nearly forty years ago when we attended preschool together at Holy Child Jesus, a tiny private school in our slightly bigger hometown. I moved away shortly after preschool and returned to our hometown just before middle school, where I was in class with Erika once again. We spent our remaining grade school years in the same classes and clubs, as well as graduated together and headed off to college at the same time. It was not until we were young adults, how-ever, that Erika and I became friends. One thing I distinctly remember about her all those years is that she was a natural leader, even at a young age.

My friend Erika always seemed to make just the right decisions. She stepped out after high school and ventured off alone to attend Dillard University in New Orleans, Louisiana. She continued to further her studies, completing several degrees along the way. She married her best friend and had two beautiful children. Her life just seemed perfect.

It was when I was given a copy of Preparing Girls for War to read that I realized how unrealistic it is to think anyone's life can be labeled as "perfect". We all face similar challenges as children, adolescents, adults, and parents. It is the choices we make during those challenging times that determine our outcomes. And that is just what Erika addresses in the book – making the right choices. But one can hardly commit to such a hardy task when you lack the proper tools of preparation. Again, Erika responds to this need by giving a suit of armor accessible to all who need it.

I am especially impressed at her poignant descriptions of sensitive subject matters such as sexually transmitted diseases and infections. Erika went there with graphic images of exactly what can happen when young people make bad choices about their bodies. She did not attempt to paint a pretty picture or create subtlety to her audience. Instead she jutted forward with the truth. More noticeable, even, is her foundation rooted in the word of God. In a time when people expend so much energy on being politically correct and inoffensive, I was elated to read a book that states it is all right for our children to believe in Christ. As a parent and mentor, I was empowered to feel I can still deliver life lessons using biblical references, yet maintain relevance.

It is with pleasure and great honor that I recommend this book to teens, friends of teens, parents of teens, and anyone else who in one way or the other impact the lives of teens today. This book concisely puts into perspective all the taboo conversations we've been hesitant to address with our teenagers. Now we have the right armor to do so.

Preface

Preface

I never thought that life would be so scary and that I would be faced with the troubles of today. As I reflect back 23 years ago, or more, I realize that I was not prepared for war. In fact, I did not know how or why I needed to be prepared. I had a great life, great parents and sort of cruised through my teenage and young adult years making some serious decisions. I made choices about my spiritual life, boyfriends, girlfriends, close associates, enemies, colleges and jobs. Some were bad choices, and I, unfortunately, had some setbacks. Some of the decisions could have ruined my life, but through God's grace and mercy, I was protected, and I made it through.

When I was 7 years old, my cousin Sharon who was 16, and her friend Tameka, 15, would babysit me for my parents. Little did my parents or I know that this would be my first exposure to cigarettes. Sharon wanted me to take a puff just to keep from telling on her. So, I tried it. Was it the right thing to do? No. Did I know better? I would like to say that I did not, but somewhere in my mind, I knew it was wrong. What would have happened to me if I had stayed surrounded by them in that environment? Would I have been subjected to other inappropriate behaviors as they were; such as marijuana, heroin, cocaine, sex trafficking or even a lesbianism? Would I have given up on life and all the wonderful things that God had planned for me? I could have lived a life of horror...living from crack house to crack house, living in alleys, selling my body for the next smoke, but I chose to live a different life. As I traveled my journey, I was frequently reminded of this scripture from (New International Version, Ephesians 2:1-5, 8).

> "[1]*As for you, you were dead in your transgressions and sins, in which you used to live when you followed the ways of this world and of the ruler of the kingdom of the air, the spirit who is now at work in those who are disobedient. All of us also lived among them at one time, gratifying the cravings of our flesh and following its thought. Like the rest, we were by nature deserving of wrath. [4]But because of his great love for us, God, who is rich in mercy, made us alive with Christ even when we were dead in transgressions- [8]For it is by grace you have been saved, through faith- and this is not from yourselves, it is the gift of God*".

There are intricate parts of our brain that control every aspect of our body. They control the way we think (prefrontal cortex), the way we feel (the limbic system) and how we respond to situations (receptors) thereby causing us to fight and battle with the flesh each and every day. We battle with negative thoughts and spirits. We battle with emotions. We battle with making the right choices and decisions. We allow the negative influences and beliefs of our friends and the people around us to take control of our lives. Nevertheless, when we know better and have the right armor to go to war (i.e. self, friends and enemies), we can live a God-filled and abundant life.

As you encounter situations throughout your life, my hope is that you can use the tools and knowledge embedded in this book to help you win the WAR!

Chapter 1

"The whole secret lies in confusing the enemy, so that
he cannot fathom our real intent."
— Sun Tzu, The Art of War

CHAPTER 1

There Is Nothing Good in Man

Meat for the Wolves

Meat for the Wolves is the conscious reality that girls are examples of sheep amongst ravenous wolves. In the book of Matthew, Christ states, *"I am sending you out like sheep among wolves. Therefore, be as shrewd as serpents and as innocent as doves"* *(Matt 10:16 NIV)*. For the context of this chapter, the sheep in this scripture represents the girls, and the wolves represent the boys. Girls are considered vulnerable, innocent, young, untrained, inexperienced, easily convinced or persuaded. The wolves are shrewd, convincing, subtle, crafty, sly, ruling nature, hypocritical, trained in the art of falsehood and deceit to get what they desire. As a young boy, society teaches the male to whisper "sweet nothings", which are meaningless words to get what he wants, in the ears of girls to persuade them to trust and like him. This art of whispering is as old as Genesis 3 when the serpent asked the woman a question about eating from the forbidden tree of knowledge. He, the serpent, knew the answer but with his sly, subtle, convincing nature the woman being intuitive wanted to touch the fruit, eat the fruit, experience the gift of the fruit but did not want to suffer the consequences of being disobedient. This is what is known as Living for the Moment and not thinking of the consequences or effects that our actions will have on tomorrow. Our blessings and our curses become activated with a word. Therefore, we must be mindful of the words whispered in our ears.

Preparing Girls for War is equipping girls with the knowledge of being more than meat for the wolves. For there is nothing good in humans, male or female. We are in a constant battle to do that which is good, but mostly submit to the nature of our lower self. We are in a constant battle with the physical self, emotional self, mental self and spiritual self to do what is good and perfect in the sight of the one's we love. The Apostle Paul writes in the book of Romans, *"For I know that good itself does not dwell in me, that is, in my sinful nature. For I have the desire to do what is good, but I cannot carry it out. For I do not do the good I want to do, but the evil I do not want to do—this I keep on doing" (Rom 7:18-19 NIV).*

Humans have a will but it is so overpowered by the lusts of flesh (Sin) that they feel helpless. Their conscience, will, reason, passion to do what is right is strong; however, the consent to do the Divine will and follow Laws is inhibited by the desires of the lower self and the inability to control the inner most parts of our being. This Divine Will and Law are of the mind which consists of the Universal Law as well as the Golden Rule.

Humans according to Apostle Paul are imprisoned with the mindset of Sin. Individuals living in this world have a difficult life because we decide to live one way, but act and do things that we absolutely despise. For we know what is right, respectful and best for us, but we can't keep ourselves from the desires of sin which sabotage our thoughts and best intentions from within and without. It is the voice of the wolves that surrounds us daily whispering, speaking and falsely prophesying into our future. These wolves are only trying to fill their own lusts and desires. It is up to you to empower yourself and make good sound decisions avoiding the whispers of the wolves.

Whispers of false promises stating that "if you sleep with me, I promise I will not hurt or leave you". Another whisper of a false promise is; "I will do anything you want if you just...." (you fill in the blank). Your decisions are such that don't result in your actions. Something continues to go wrong deep within you and gets the better of your mind and heart at all times. It begins to happen so frequently that you become predictable and immune to do what is right and good for yourself and humanity. You begin to lose the trust and respect of the ones you love as well as the ones you are becoming physically, emotionally, mentally and spiritually tied too. These feelings are elevated by the inner man who knows what is right, but dwells in the darkness of your thoughts. It takes in the soul, that is, the seat of feelings, emotions, and desires delighting in the pleasures of this world and the lower self. These feelings lead to wrongful and undesirable acts stronger than the "Will" of the mind. It captures your every thought regardless of the protest, the fight, and the will to do what is right in the mind. The moment you decide to do good, sin is there to trip you up. You must show delight in doing what is right and stand firm to deny the false prophesy of the wolves dressed in sheep clothing.

Every person's need is already buried within the inner most parts of their being. These needs are dormant until activated or awakened by some-thing or some-one in its environment. You may have a need to be around others, a need to fit in and be accepted, a need for conversation, a need for laughter, a need for love, a need for affection, a need for money or a need for beautiful things. Any one of these needs can lead to the desire to listen to the wolves and their deceitful whispers.

When you have tried everything to stop being meat for the wolves, change your current situation, silence the whisperers of false promises and getting disappointed from the deceitfulness of man then you are truly prepared for war. You are sheep in the midst of wolves at the end of your rope. Is there any help for you? The answer is yes. Protect yourself with truth, righteousness, preparation of the word, salvation, prayer and offers of supplication with all your heart, mind, soul and strength to the Most High. You must renew your mind to that of the anointed and operate under a new power and authority. It is a new life and you are a new creature in the Spirit of Life in Christ. This Spirit will wash you with the Blood and cleanse you with Fire aimed at purifying your thoughts and forgiving you of your past transgressions.

Preparing Girls for War teaches you to learn from past experiences and gives you a testimony to help other girls in every humanly possible ways to win their personal battles. Learning and growing from these individual battles are small but they strengthen your faith and you to become victorious in the War against the Prince of the Powers of the Air and his soldiers. These soldiers are the sheep in wolves clothing. Victory over the Prince and his soldiers makes you Master of your Fate and Captain of your Soul. Hence, kill your wolf with the silver bullet of accepting the alive and present anointed spirit living within you that will drown out the whispers of the Prince and his sons and awaken the inward man called the Comforter that Spirit of Truth. In the book of John chapter 14 verse 23, Christ, the Anointed, said,

"Anyone who loves me will obey my teaching (the law). My Father (The Most High) will love you, and we

(Christ and The Most High) will come to you and make their home inside you."

Christ goes on to say in John 14: 26 that the Advocate, The Comforter, the Holy Spirit, the Spirit of Truth, whom the Most High will send in the name of Christ, the Anointed, will teach you all things and will remind you of everything the Spirit of Christ has taught you in your heart, mind and soul. So you are not alone in your war. You have the Spirit of The Most High, The Spirit of Christ and The Spirit of Truth to help you make good decisions in bringing victory in your war.

by Dr. Clayton Gibson, III

Chapter 2

"Victorious warriors win first and then go to war, while defeated warriors go to war first and then seek to win"
— Sun Tzu, The Art of War

CHAPTER 2

Spiritual War Is Real

God's Viewpoint on the Choices We Make

Was I equipped to prepare Latoya for the battle that could destroy her life? Often, we battle with making sound decisions. We battle with what our heart is saying, what our friends are saying and what a host of significant others are saying. We straddle the fence with our choices because we are not fully versed on the will of God. In the early spring of 2015, I remember having a conversation with a little girl, named Latoya, who was 10 years old in the sixth grade. I met her during a speaking engagement with a youth group in Atlanta. She appeared to be quite outspoken. She walked up to me and said, "Dr. Gibson, I really liked your chat with our group. I have been battling with making decisions in my life. May I ask your opinion about something?" With open arms, I knew that if she had the courage to ask for my opinion, I needed to take the time to speak with her. Of course, nothing could have prepared me for what I was about to hear. Latoya said to me, "My mother is lesbian, and I asked her how I would know if

I am lesbian too? My mother told me that I needed to try it for myself to determine if it was for me. I want to try it". What do you think, Dr. Gibson?" My heart was immediately broken, and I was at a loss for words, but I remembered that I needed to be the one to give her the tools to make the best decision.

I took a deep breath and said, "You know, in the Holy Bible, the book of Leviticus Chapter 20:13, says, *13If a man lies with a male as with a woman, both of them have committed an abomination; an action that is vicious or vile; an action that arouses disgust or abhorrence; they shall surely be put to death; their blood is upon them.*" She looked at me and said, "So are you saying that God does not want girls to date girls and boys to date boys?" I said "Yes"! This is exactly what I mean. Tears came to my eyes, and I knew at that point, she just needed the right tools to fight the battle she was about to tackle. She was completely unaware of what God's expectations are for her life. She needed to have a solid foundation based on sound principles.

Many of you are battling a spiritual war. You are in the midst of fighting the evil spirits that intervene in human affairs. You are trying to determine whether you are making the right decisions about homosexuality, premarital sex, drinking, using illegal drugs and following the rules provided by your parents and others in authority. Well, just as I shared the appropriate tools with Latoya, I would like to provide you with my best spiritual weapon for making intelligent decisions. You see, in today's society, we have the right to decide our sexual preferences and companions. Many Americans disagree with same sex marriages and strange as it may seem, several will disagree with the partners you have chosen of the opposite gender. Does that matter? May be. Does God have an opinion about either? Sure he does. The book of 2 Corinthians 6:14 states that,

"14Be ye not unequally yoked together with unbelievers: for what fellowship hath righteousness with unrighteousness? And what communion hath light with darkness"?

Hebrews 13:4 states, *"4Let marriage be held in honor among all, and let the marriage bed be undefiled, for God will judge the sexually immoral and adulterous".*

Despite how the government has passed the law around gay relationships, you will continue to face discrimination by society. The judgements against you will require that you to have a firm foundation and be ready to fight the war. *Remember, if you are a believer and follower of Christ, these words can help you.*

What does the Holy Bible say about homosexuality?

The first mention of homosexuality appeared at the beginning of the Old Testament:

- *The wicked men of Sodom attempted a homosexual rape of two messengers from God who had come to visit Lot. As a result of this and other widespread wickedness, God destroyed the cities of Sodom and Gomorrah with a storm of fire and brimstone (Genesis 19:1-13).*

The next two verses are in Leviticus

- *You shall not lie with a male as with a woman. It is an abomination. (NKJV, Leviticus 18:22)*

- *If a man lies with a male as he lies with a woman, both of them have committed an abomination (a vile, shameful, or detestable action, condition, habit). They shall surely be put to death. Their blood shall be upon them. (NKVJ, Leviticus 20:13)*

In the New Testament, Jesus condemned all forms of sexual immorality:

- *What comes out of you is what defiles you. For from within, out of your hearts, come evil thoughts, sexual immorality, theft, murder, adultery, greed, malice, deceit, lewdness, envy, slander, arrogance and folly. All these evils come from inside and defile you. (TNIV, Mark 7:20-23)*

2But because of the temptation to sexual immorality, each man should have his own wife and each woman her own husband (1 Corinthians 7:2).

I do not want you to think that just because you are homosexual, bisexual, or lesbian that there is anything wrong with you as a person. However, I do want you to reflect into your past or dig deep into your subconscious to determine whether you are reacting to a past traumatic experience that you have repressed or perhaps this is a learned behavior. Choosing this lifestyle from a spiritual perspective simply means that you have chosen a lifestyle that is not pleasing to GOD. You have decided to defy what is known to be against the will of our most Heavenly One. You have decided to satisfy your flesh and succumb to what the devil wants you to do. You see, we all have choices; some choices are made from impulse, hurt, anger or clearly the lack of knowledge. In the Christian world, sexual immorality is unique. It is all sex outside of a legitimate marriage in God's sight. It's not just practicing homosexuality. It is any sin against one's own body.

Sexual Immorality can bring a lot of regret, pain and shame. Seek out those like a Psychologist, or Licensed Counselor who can help you understand why you have chosen this lifestyle.

It is most important to make sure that you love yourself. The book of Proverbs 19:8, says,

"8To acquire wisdom is to love oneself; people who cherish understanding will prosper. It also tells you to love yourself and your neighbor".

Whoever you are, whatever you are identified as, you are human, and you are a beloved creation of whatever God or higher power that you believe in is out there. He made you so He could love you, and love you He shall, no matter what, and no matter how you find Him. Be kind to yourself, and love yourself. It is easier to love something or someone else if you love yourself fully. It is all right if it takes you a long time to find this love within yourself.

The spiritual war is very real. People might tell you that you are wrong for believing, even call you names for what you believe. This is where the love of God can help. We are not perfect. Though we are created in God's image, we are only human. The only thing about us that is perfect is our immortal souls. The love of something greater than yourself can remind you that even though those around you may not be perfect, they too can still be loved.

The path to finding this love can be a difficult one filled with hardships. Your faith may be tested. It is during these times that you must surround yourself with like-minded family and friends. Ask those who have a strong sense of faith. Consult your spiritual leader. It may be your pastor, priest or shaman. Do not go at it alone.

What does the Holy Bible say about pre-marital sex?

- *[20]"but should write to them to abstain from the things polluted by idols, and from sexual immorality, and from what has been strangled, and from blood" (Acts 15:20).*

- *[13]"Food is meant for the stomach and the stomach for food"—and God will destroy both one and the other. The body is not meant for sexual immorality, but for the Lord, and the Lord for the body" (1 Corinthians 6:13).*

Don't Be A "Car Charger" for Boys

Will I allow him to use me as an outlet? Can he just plug in when he gets ready? Teenage boys often are more concerned with sex than actual relationships. That is not necessarily a bad thing, as this is the age where both boys and girls are likely to explore their sexuality. However, some boys make games of it, trying to have sex with as many girls as they can. Some might only pick one girl but will try to keep stringing her along for as long as they can. Now, I am not saying all boys this age are like that, but many of them are, and you should try to be aware of them.

It can be difficult to tell sometimes. Maybe he will tell you he loves you but is not ready for a relationship. Maybe you two agreed to be "friends with benefits." Neither of these is ideal, nor healthy. Boys who say they love you but never want to do anything more than have sex with you may be taking advantage of your feelings. Try to avoid this type of relationship. If he actually loves you, he will stay even if you say "NO" to sex.

The friend with benefits type of relationship is just as unhealthy as the previous type, though sometimes it is a different kind of unhealthiness. You may think, this will not be so bad. We are not in a relationship, so there will not be any messy breakup or worry about them cheating. That is not entirely true. I could even argue that "friends with benefits" is messier than a relationship. You do not necessarily know if they are having sex with someone else at the same time as you. Maybe you agreed to tell each other about other partners, but they may not respect that. You might think that there are no emotions in a "friends with benefits" relationship, but you would be wrong. You need to have some kind of attraction to start with, even if it is just a physical one. The act of sex is a very intimate one, and things like that can easily lead to ideas of and desires for romance instead of just sex. Often, this ends up one-sided, and one person ends up with a broken heart. This is also something you should try to avoid entirely. The trust that is there in an actual relationship is not always there in a friends with benefits relationship. You do not know if they are telling the truth about their history if you even thought to ask.

Girls, you are more than just a toy for boys to play with. You are a human being, and easily their equal.

This also means you should not use boys just for sex, either. No one deserves that, and is it not said, "Do unto others as you would have them do to you"? Respect for yourself and for the people around you are important to have in all aspects of your life. There may be some people whom you think do not deserve that respect. There are some terrible people out there, but you do not need to associate yourself with them.

How do I respond when my boyfriend wants me to have sex?

Just say "No". You have that right. Ofcourse your hormones are raging and you are having these internal feelings, but please remember, you hold all the cards. Tell him that you would like to wait until you get married and let him know that your body is your most precious possession and that you are not ready to share it with him. Let him know that there is a level of commitment that you expect. If he respects your feelings, he will understand. If his behavior changes, this may be a good indication that he is not with you for the right reasons. It is all about setting *standards* for yourself!

If I have already had a sexual relationship with my boyfriend, how can I stop the sexual relationship and continue to keep him attracted to me?

You have the right just to say NO MORE! You do not owe anyone an explanation. However, if you are inclined to communicate why your decision has changed, tell him that you made your previous decision based on emotions and not on the will of GOD. If he was truly attracted to you for more than just the sex, he would continue the relationship. Remember, this is indicative of how he feels about you and the relationship.

If I have sex with him, will he tell his "boys" and what will they think about me?

Depending on the guy, he may share it with others. Many young men like to share their sexual exploits with their friends. You should be aware of this. Some may think of you as the girl who puts out or is "easy". Twenty-five sexually active boys between the ages of 16 and 19 were polled about sharing their sexual encounters, and 92% of those polled reported that they shared their sexual encounters with all of their guy friends or at least the guys who they considered themselves to be close with. Of the sexually active boys, 90% of them states that they were not looking for a serious relationship with the girls that they had sex with.

Christianity is not the only path to take. There are various ways you can fight the spiritual war, even if you do not believe in a higher power. Maybe you do not believe in God right now, but you might find that through the path of spirituality you can find guidance and the help you might otherwise have been lacking. Guidance can come from instructors, pastors, mentors, your family doctor, counselors at school, siblings, an aunt or uncle.

There is a wealth of support from various religious backgrounds such as Christianity, Catholicism, Jehovah Witness, Islamic or Hinduism. You can always find someone to guide you.

"For what is done or learned by one class of women becomes, by virtue of their common womanhood, the property of all women."
—Elizabeth Blackwell
(The first woman in the U.S. to become a physician)

Health Consequences as A Result of Your Choices

What are some of the risks of having pre-marital sex?

When making adult decisions such as pre-marital sex, you stand a risk of acquiring various sexually transmitted diseases (STDs) and sexually transmitted infections (STIs). Sexual contact includes kissing, oral-genital contact, genital-genital contact, and the use of sexual toys shared by another, such as toys designed for both partners.

In 2011, I remember showing up at my office a little later than usual, and one of the Directors was waiting on me. She had a very upset employee who had just been notified by her daughter's doctor that her 14-year-old daughter's test results showed that she was HIV-positive. She had been having sex with someone she trusted and thought she loved, only to find out that he had had sex with 3 other young ladies who were all HIV-positive now. Although being HIV-positive is not a death sentence, it comes with lifelong consequences and roadblocks like ongoing doctor visits, future dating and family planning, and a very high risk of developing more serious diseases due to a compromised immune system.

There are many sexually transmitted diseases that you can acquire that may cause other chronic diseases or can kill you as a result of the decisions you make. Proper precautions, such as *always* using a condom when you have sex, can help avoid these. If you do end up contracting one of the many sexually transmitted diseases or infections, seek counseling and treatment from your doctor immediately. There is some form of treatment for all and a cure for many. Even if you are unsure of whether you have contracted a sexually transmitted infection (STI) or sexually transmitted disease (STD), ask your doctor to test you just in case. Any time you change sexual partners, make sure to ask them about their history and if they may have ever been infected with a disease. Remember to check yourself after and during sexual relationships. Some of these STIs and STDs include the following (Centers for Disease and Control and Prevention (CDC, 2015) / Wikipedia):

Herpes Simplex Virus is a common sexually transmitted infection that affects boys, girls, men and women.

There is no cure for herpes. If infected, you can be contagious even if you have no visible sores. Herpes simplex type 1, which is transmitted through oral secretions or sores on the skin, can be spread through kissing or sharing objects such as toothbrushes or eating utensils. The herpes simplex virus type 1 (HSV-1) is a non-sexually transmitted infection that many people have, often seen in the form of cold sores, and is not likely to cause adverse health problems. It is still possible to contract genital herpes from the type 1 virus but is much less common than the type 2, and an open sore must be present to spread through type one. The herpes simplex virus type 2 (HSV-2) is the strain that causes genital herpes. Sexual contact is the primary medium for transmitting the type 2 virus. After the initial infection, the virus lies dormant in your body and can reactivate several times a year. The only way to avoid STDs is not to have vaginal, anal, or oral sex. If you are sexually active, you can lower your chances of getting herpes by being in a long-term mutually monogamous relationship with a partner who has been tested and has negative STD test results; using latex condoms the right way every time you have sex.

Just remember, you may never know if your sexual partner has this disease unless they divulge the information to you, so be smart about your decision when choosing a partner.

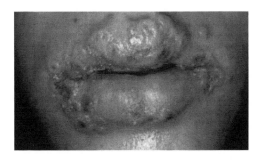

Picture by K. Salaris

Human Immunodeficiency Virus (HIV). HIV is a virus spread through certain body fluids via sexual contact (secretions), sharing needles to inject drugs or in saloon, mother to baby during pregnancy, birth or breastfeeding. HIV attacks the body's immune system, specifically the CD4 cells, often called T cells. Once the human immunodeficiency virus (HIV) enters your body, it launches a direct attack on your immune system. Over time, HIV can destroy so many of these cells that the body can't fight off infections and disease About 50,000 people are infected with HIV each year, and one in four is 13 to 24 years old. Youth make up

7% of the more than 1 million people in the US living with HIV. About 12,000 youths were infected with HIV in 2010. The greatest number of infections occurred among gay and bisexual youths. Your risk of contracting HIV is when you start having sex or start injecting drugs. The best option for avoiding contracting HIV/AID is abstinence, but if you are at risk, be sure to use condoms the right way every time you have anal or vaginal sex. Always think smart by limiting your number of sex partners and don't inject drugs, or if you do, don't share needles (CDC 2015 Fast Fact Sheet).

Acquired immunodeficiency syndrome (AIDS) is an advanced stage of infection with the human immunodeficiency virus. HIV usually is spread from person to person through contact with infected fluids or blood.

Human papillomavirus is the most common sexually transmitted infection. You can get HPV by having vaginal, anal, or oral sex with someone who has the virus. It is most commonly spread during vaginal or anal sex. HPV can be transmitted even when an infected person show no signs or symptoms. Anyone who is sexually active can get HPV, even if you have had sex with only one person. You also can develop symptoms years after you have sex with someone who is infected making it difficult to know when you first became infected. In most cases, HPV goes away on its own and does not cause any health problems. But when HPV does not go away, it can cause health problems such as genital warts and cancer.

Genital warts usually appear as a small bump or group of bumps in the genital area. They can be small or large, raised or flat, or shaped like a cauliflower. A healthcare provider can usually diagnose warts by looking at the genital area.

Hepatitis B is a virus that infects the liver. The highest concentrations of HBV are found in blood, with lower concentrations found in other body fluids including wound exudates, semen, vaginal secretions, and saliva. You can have hepatitis B and not know it. You may not have symptoms. You may get hepatitis B if you:

- have sex with an infected person without using a condom,

- share needles (used for injecting drugs) with an infected person,
- get a tattoo or piercing with tools that weren't sterilized, or
- share personal items such as razors or toothbrushes with an infected person.

Gonorrhea is most commonly spread during sex. It is an infection caused by a sexually transmitted bacterium that can infect both males and females. Gonorrhea most often affects the urethra, rectum or throat. In females, gonorrhea can also infect the cervix and fallopian tubes. Gonorrhea is treatable like all STIs and is even curable.

Syphilis is a bacterial infection usually spread by sexual contact. The disease starts as a painless sore typically on your genitals, rectum or mouth. Syphilis spreads from person to person via skin or mucous membrane contact with these sores. After the initial infection, the syphilis bacteria can lie dormant in your body for decades before becoming active again. Syphilis is another treatable disease, best treated early on. If you think you might have anything, talk to your doctor. They will be able to diagnose and help you get treatment.

Pregnancy. While this isn't an STI or STD, as a female having unprotected sex, predisposes you to risk. If you are a married woman trying to have a child, know you both want and are ready for children and have discussed it previously, then by all means, do so. However, if none of that has occurred, and you are unmarried, pregnancy from unprotected sex is a very real risk. If you have sex without a condom, and are not on birth control or using some secondary form of contraceptive, the risk of getting pregnant is *extremely high.* Even if you use some other form of contraceptive, the risk of unplanned pregnancy is still very high. If you know you are not ready for a child, then use a condom. When you have sex, you are saying that you are old enough and responsible enough for such decisions, therefore, saying you are old enough and responsible enough for the consequences of such decisions. If you know you are not ready for these yet, then think about the decisions you may be making, or may be thinking of making, first.

Maybe you are a believer of a religion that speaks against pre-marital sex and you still choose to have sex. Be sure to be responsible and practice safe sex. Always use a condom. Don't ever let your partner, male or female, convince you otherwise. Even if you're on birth control, you can still end up pregnant. Even if you think "It can't happen to me," it most certainly can. While there are other forms of contraceptives aside from the condom, the condom is the most effective form of contraceptive when used correctly. Remember, your body is your temple. If you do not cherish and treat your body the way you should, no one else will.

It is also worthy of note that, there is no such thing as "safe" sex. The only truly effective way to completely prevent STDs is ABSTINENCE! The choice you make today can dictate your tomorrow!

I'm pregnant. Now what?

Many of us are judged on the choices we make. From a Christian's perspective, it is important to know that it is not a sin to be pregnant out of wedlock, but it is a sin to have sex outside the marriage relationship—and it is just as much a sin for the boy as for the girl. When you are having sexual relationships, it is much easier to hide from critical eyes until your pregnancy becomes obvious. Once you become pregnant, this now becomes more embarrassing for you and to your family's reputation in the Christian Community. As disappointing and overwhelming as it may be to learn that you are pregnant, it's essential to keep focused and your spirit high. The damage is done. The decision you made to have sex cannot be avoided now. This new situation is not about the morality of out-of-wedlock sex, what your friends are going to say, what your teachers are thinking, what your church family thinks or the reputation of your family. It's about the development of a child. All children are blessings from God, and He has a plan for each one (Psalm 139:13-18). New King James Version (NKJV)

"13 For You formed my inward parts; You covered me in my mother's womb. 14 I will praise You, for I am fearfully and wonderfully made; Marvelous are Your works, And that my soul knows very well. 15 My frame was not hidden from You, When I was made in secret, And skillfully wrought in the lowest parts of the earth. 16 Your eyes saw my substance, being yet unformed. And in Your book they all were written, The days fashioned for me, When as yet there were none of them. 17 How precious also are Your thoughts to me, O God! How great is the sum of them! 18 If I should count them, they would be more in number than the sand; When I awake, I am still with You".

Even if the circumstances in which the baby comes are less than ideal, that child is as precious and loved by God as any others. Many challenges and changes await you and your family's life. Life is no longer all about you. It's about the baby you bring into the world. You may start to think, will I have to drop out of school? Will my parents and family help me take care of my baby? What will I do to financially support my baby as a teen? Will I become just another statistic of Welfare Assistance? What if my baby is born with a special needs disorder, who will help me with him or her? How and where will I find resources to help my baby? There are no clear cut answers for the many of these questions, but it is very important to immediately develop a plan once your pregnancy has been confirmed.

What's My Plan?

1. Create a channel of communication with your parents, family, friends or mentor to build a supportive structure.

2. Determine if you are going to abort, put the baby up for adoption or prepare for parental planning.

   a. If you are thinking about aborting, consider any religious beliefs that you have. Make sure that you have thought this decision through. Don't make a decision off of impulse or fear of what others think. You need to seek counseling so that you will understand any possible physical and emotional effects and risks associated with an abortion.

   b. If you are thinking about putting the baby up for adoption, make sure that you have thought this decision through. Seek counseling to understand your options and any emotions that you may encounter in the future from an adoption

3. If you are thinking about planning to be a single mother, seek a healthcare provider to assist you

with prenatal care and work with a counselor to help you locate local resources for a safe and healthy pregnancy.

4. Stay focused and in school to ensure that you are prepared to assist with building a future for you and your child.

5. Seek a part-time job after school to save money and to begin your journey on becoming responsible.

6. Upon graduation from high school, plan to go to college or seek to get a trade to ensure a better life for you and your baby.

7. After delivery, talk with your doctor about birth control and learn from your past.

Just remember, it's not about you anymore. It's about the baby! Having the support of a parent, guardian or other trusted adults can make a huge difference.

How does drinking alcohol and using illegal substances affect my body?

Alcohol and illegal drugs can cause depression and hallucinations, not to mention they are completely unhealthy and can cause adverse health effects. If you are hanging with your friends and think that smoking and drinking alcohol with them is cool, know that it affects almost every part of your body negatively.

- Drugs and alcohol affect the way you think, making it harder to make safe choices and protect yourself in dangerous situations.

- Drug and alcohol use can lead to unhealthy sexual practices, such as having sex before you are ready or not asking if your partner has a sexually transmitted infection. Or you may have sex without using a condom, which can put you at risk for getting STIs or pregnancy.

- Sharing needles and other equipment for injecting drugs can spread Hepatitis, HIV and other dangerous infections.

- Drugs are not meant to be in your body. You could become very sick or die.

- Be aware of the people you may be around. Be aware of how much alcohol you may be ingesting, if you choose to. Be aware of your limits. Make it a rule to stay clear of illegal or drugs not prescribed for you. Don't allow friends to pressure you into anything you are not comfortable with doing. You get to decide who you let into your inner circle. If the circle you are surrounded by makes bad decisions, then find a new inner circle.

Obeying Those in Authority

It is important to obey those in authority like your parents, legal guardians, teachers, grandparents. A good relationship with your parents or those in authority is a good thing to have. Listening to your parents may sound like a dopey thing. You may even think that they are "old school" and have no idea what growing up is like, but in reality, they do and want you to avoid the mistakes that they made during their young years. Open communication is very important and should go both ways. When you are disturbed about a situation that may pertain to the rules prescribed by those in authority, you should sit and talk with them to understand their reasoning behind the decision that has been made. You benefit by listening to them and earning their trust. They become more lenient and begin to trust you with more things, believing you are smart enough to do the right thing. It shows them that you are a responsible young adult and they appreciate it even if they may not always say so. Talk to them when you are unsure. They are able to provide you with the right answers or direct you to someone with the correct answers. Your parents are there for you unconditionally. They are the channel to your existence they love you. Your parents are not the enemy. It breaks their heart to fight with you. They do not like to punish you and only use it to show their love for you. When you run into a problem, your parents are there to help and support you through any situation. Parents mean well and only want what is best for you. Sometimes, your parents may not believe the things you tell them because they may have observed your past or because your story doesn't add up. For instance, when I was in high school, one of my friends was bullied terribly. She had a bad relationship with her parents, and they didn't believe her when she told them about it. I know that sounds awful, but it happened. So instead, my friend told one of her favorite teachers, who in turn talked to her parents. They believed her then. This may not sound helpful, but think for a moment. Sometimes, a bad relationship with your parents is inevitable, but it really helps to try to have a good one with them. It will make you happier in the long run, too. Your parents/guardian and those in authority are usually dear people, and there none like them. They really do love you.

Chapter 3

Supreme excellence consists of breaking the enemy's
resistance without fighting."
— Sun Tzu, The Art of War

CHAPTER 3

Can I Win the Physical War or Will the Mental Game Overrule?

Coping with Bullies/Enemies

Physical war is something I would never wish on my worst enemy. When I was in grade school, I was bullied by my first cousin, Rachel. It was one of the worst feelings. Whenever I would disagree with her or didn't do what she wanted me to, she would start a fight with me after school. This went on for three years. I would literally be sick to my stomach knowing that this girl who seemed at that time to be the jolly green giant in my class would be waiting for me when I walked out of the school gates. I would pretend to be sick right after lunch and have the teacher call my father to pick me up early just to avoid being jumped. Until one day, my sister spilled the beans. She told our dad that I was being bullied by Rachel. Now, this had been going on for years and he had always taught me to turn the other cheek. This particular day, he picked me up from school and took me home. He told me that I could no longer call him from work pretending to be sick because I was afraid. He said he would teach me how to defend myself. This was unusual because he was the one who always taught us to turn the other cheek. Of course, had he taught me this a long time before, I could have avoided getting beaten up for three years. He taught me how to fight. My father warned me again that I had better defend myself or I would have to answer to him. At this point, I was physically ready to take Rachel on, but in my head, I thought this girl will smash me like potatoes. But, I knew that I had to go to war.

The war was on! The next day after school, she was waiting for me outside the gates. She and a group of other kids were walking behind me. As we approached the street I lived on, she pushed me from behind. Yes, I was afraid, but I immediately turned around and gave her all I had. All I could remember hearing was my father's voice saying, if you don't get her, I'm going to get you when you get home. So, I fought her. I remember Mr. Willie, the man who manned the laundromat, coming out to break up the fight up. Mr. Willie was telling me to let her go. I was still fighting and saying, "No, I have to get her good, because if I don't my father is going to get me when I get home."

The fight was over and I felt like Mohammed Ali. Little did I know, this physical war was over. I needed to stand up for myself. Reflecting back, I could have handled the situation differently. I should have told my father, the principle and a teacher earlier how I was being bullied so that they could have stepped in and helped. Now that I am older, I understand the basic psychology of a bully. Bullies tend to attack others emotionally to empower themselves. That is what Rachel was doing, seeking power. She may have been insecure about herself. I should have taken her bullying power away by not allowing it to affect me negatively. I should have never responded to her by allowing her to torment me. It would have been easier for me to laugh at her and walk away.

What are the repercussions of handling this on my own?

Handling a bullying situation by yourself sounds like a good idea, right? Fight back, maybe give them a punch or two in the face. Get back at them however they've been bullying you. This might not always be such a good idea. Maybe those who have taught you about standing up to bullies tell you to fight back. Sometimes, this can escalate the situation. What started as verbal bullying can escalate into physical bullying. No forms of bullying are pleasant, and all can be scarring. Sometimes, fighting back will work the opposite and make the bully meaner than before.

Maybe you tried to talk to the bully first and that didn't work. Bullying someone back who is bullying you is *never* the right thing to do. It brings you down to their level, and makes you feel terrible. Bullying someone back is never the right direction to go.

Second, fighting back physically can get you in trouble. You could end up with detention or suspension from school, to having a criminal record. A criminal record can cause many problems for you in the future, even if it's just for an offense so minimal, or if it's a juvenile record. It can limit your chances of securing a job, travelling, or trying to find a place to rent, or buying. These things are all pretty essential.

Jasmin was 17 years old and had been bullied for two and a half years by one of her classmates. She never told a person of authority but realized that she was going to take matters into her own hands. One summer evening in her hometown, Jasmin heard a rock hit her mother's living room window. She looked out of the window and realized that it was the bully who had taunted her for years. She decided right then that the bullying had to stop and that she was going to be the one to stop it. Jasmin took a kitchen knife and ran outside to put a stop to what she thought would be the end of her bullying escapade. However, it turned out to be the beginning of a real war. She stabbed her bully, killing her. Jasmin is now serving a life sentence in prison. This is serious business. What could have easily been handled by authorities turned into a life of terror for her and her family.

Being bullied is a very real problem for many children and young adults. People are bullied for several reasons and in several ways, both physically and psychologically. The only way to make it stop is to take away the bully's power. Many circumstances can turn a person into a bully, and sometimes, it might just be the person. Standing by can be just as bad; watching as another person is picked on or teased meanly by another and not doing anything about it. Maybe you don't want to get directly involved. There are other ways you can still help. You can find a teacher, or adult or authority figure of some kind. Tell them what's happening, and let them know where. You can talk to the person being bullied afterward, and try to help them find an authority figure of some kind so they can tell them what had happened, or what has been going on.

To bully a bully back is never the right path to thread. If you or someone you know is being bullied, revenge is never the right thing to do. It might feel good at that moment, but you'll regret it later. You'll feel bad because that's not how you are. If you are being bullied, you can tell them to stop. Don't ask them, tell them. Tell them firmly that you've had enough and they need to stop now. If that doesn't work, find an authority figure like a teacher, your parents, an adult or even a friend who is older than you, tell them. Tell someone; explain to them what has been happening. Ask for help. It is unhealthy to keep it all bottled up inside. There will always be someone you can confide in if you don't want anyone else to know just yet, or at all. Even if you don't think it will help, talk to someone about it. You'd be surprised at how much even just talking about something can help you. Even if you don't do anything at that point other than talk, it can be incredibly helpful to you and your mental and emotional health. When it comes to mental health and bullying, this is very, very important.

Overcoming Bad Decisions

Learning to forgive yourself is one of the hardest things to do. There are many times in life where you will be faced with choices. These choices will test your morals and your trust. For instance, you are hanging out with friends one day and one of your friends pulls out illegal drugs. It may be marijuana, amphetamines, or ecstasy. You can choose here whether to take up smoking or use this drug. But one little puff or swallow of a pill can't hurt, right? Wrong. Maybe you won't get addicted right then and there, but you might. Maybe it won't be the determining factor in whether you get lung cancer later in life, but it might. Decisions like that may run rampant throughout your lives, and sometimes you don't even notice them.

There was a girl I knew named Tanya. She was born in prison and given to her aunt three days following her birth. She lived with her aunt from 3 days old until the age of 12. At the age of 12, Tanya was given back to her mother who was released from prison and began to experience a hard life. She lived from house to house, fell in with the wrong crowd and would drink unhealthy amounts of alcohol on a fairly regular basis. She even did hard drugs occasionally. She was molested by her uncle and a friend of the family and was never told that this was an unacceptable behavior. It became a part of the norm for her. She enjoyed the sexual encounters and began to seek out other experiences with different men. This became an addiction, which led to her being used by a pimp for sex trafficking where she could make money for both him and her. She began to make money, still not understanding that this was wrong and illegal. Until one day, she was picked up by police officers and had to sit before a judge. Because she was underage, the judge required that she seek treatment and counseling to help her understand and overcome this addiction. After multiple admits to treatment, Tanya was able to realize and modify her behavior. She admitted to making a lot of choices that, if given the opportunity, she would go back and choose very differently. Since treatment and months of therapy, Tanya has stayed away from the drugs, marijuana, and sex trafficking.

Often, making decisions like that can lead to any number of bad situations. While this is an extreme case, a lot of small bad decisions can quickly lead up to that.

We can assume your parents, or some authoritative figures, have taught you the difference of right from wrong, and that you have some set base of morals. That is a good thing to have even though you may doubt yourself sometimes. When that doubt arises, trust yourself. Trust yourself to know you can make the right choice. Say no to that cigarette they offer. Say no to that drink they try to shove in your hands, especially if you are underage. Say no to that joint, to the needle, to the pills, the powder or the liquid substances. Say no to being sexually abused. If you ever think you are in a bad situation, trust yourself to make the right choices. More often than not, if you do not give in to temptation or let yourself be pressured into anything, you have made the right decision.

What if you have made the wrong decision? What if you started smoking, for instance? All is certainly not lost. Put down the cigarette and pick up a new hobby. As hard as quitting is, distracting yourself with something that you love can be a life changer. If it does not help you, there are all types of ways to help you quit. Maybe that wrong choice was something else entirely. That is okay, too. You are human. You are not perfect. It is impossible to be perfect, and no one is expecting you to. You may be clouded by doubts, worry, and emotions that can sometimes betray you. You are not beyond help, no matter what you might think. If you have made bad decisions, you need to learn to forgive yourself. Forgive yourself for whatever choice you made. Forgive yourself for the drink, the smoke, sexual promiscuity, the fact you cheated on that test and learn from it. You are not perfect. If you can learn to forgive yourself, realizing that it may not have been entirely your fault, or if it was knowing that you learned from it and became a better person for it, you may find you are a happier person. You cannot force forgiveness, and trying to force it will not help. It may take time, so taking that time is beneficial. Analyze what happened, and forgive yourself, bit by bit.

Chapter 4

"A busy, vibrant, goal-oriented woman is so much more attractive than a woman who waits around for a man to validate her existence."
— Mandy Hale, The Single Woman: Life, Love, and a Dash of Sass

CHAPTER 4

Setting Standards for Yourself

What I Wear Matters!

Standards are something you might find yourself wondering about. Are my standards too high? Too low? How do I know what kind of standards I need to set for myself? All kinds of different images and ideas are shoved at you from a very young age, telling us to be a certain way and set out standards a certain way, and if we don't look like this or do this then we're wrong and need to change. That's not right, but we don't often realize it until it's too late.

You wonder what is okay to wear on a daily basis. Between the media, schools, parents, friends, and everything around you, you're getting a pretty conflicted message. The media tells you to dress one way, but your parents won't let you out of the house in those clothes. Your friends say that outfit is super cute, but the school won't let you wear it because it exposes too much. Things like that are very common and they make it difficult to know just what to do. There are ways to simplify this, though some people might find it boring. Dressing a certain way is more about self-respect than anything else. You're growing into a woman, and you're told to dress like one. What exactly qualifies as dressing like a "woman"? Is it skirts and high heels, dresses and sandals, jeans and sneakers? The answer is all of it. Of course, you can dress how you want, and you should try to dress with some self-respect. Typically, boys are not just attracted to one type of girl. They are attracted to all types of girls. What you wear may capture a guy's attention, but the question is, will it keep his attention? Your self-respect and self-confidence are most likely to win him over. Unfortunately, some young men may try to take advantage of the way you dress if you expose too much. If you wear short shorts and a crop top, you may be labeled as a slut. If you wear turtlenecks and jeans, you're a prude. You can't win in other people's eyes, but those people do not matter. They're the wrong kind of people to be around, and the wrong kind of people to let their opinions matter. It can be hard to break away from toxicity like that, but it is possible.

Consequently, there is nothing wrong with dressing more on the conservative side. Instead of wearing a skirt that only just covers your rear, try something that goes to your knees. The look is more versatile and you are likely to attract the right kind of attention. Try a shirt with sleeves and a sweetheart cut instead of the plunging V and spaghetti straps. There are all kinds of ways to look good without exposing your body. Looking classy is always better than looking easy.

How Can Social Media Destroy My Future?

Using social media such as Facebook, Twitter, Tumblr, Kik and Instagram is fun. You can keep connected with friends, your favorite artists and actors, find out the latest news and trends with the click of a button. Social media can also be dangerous. Social media makes it easy for bullies to have a new outlet and for sexual predators to take advantage of you. They can see everything you post online, and nitpick anything they might see wrong. Cyber-bullying is just as real a problem as bullying out in the real world. It may even be more prominent, because cyber-bullying gives the bully a different kind of power. Behind a screen, they are more anonymous. They have less worry of consequence from behind a screen.

That is not the only thing, though. If you have a job and you're on Facebook or other social media sites, your boss can likely search you up and see everything you post. They can see what you say about them, about work, your friends and family. They can see if you are actually out sick or if you're just blowing off work. They can see what you were up to on your weekend off. Anything you put up on the Internet no longer is private, no matter what you do. If it's there, someone can see it.

Think about what to post up on social media before you post it. If you just took a sexy picture in your bra, do you really think it's appropriate to post it online? Think about who might be able to see it. If a friend comments on it or likes it, one of their friends might be able to see it. This can go until complete strangers are able to see your profile, if they weren't already able to. Whether it's a picture or a status or something else, someone you don't want seeing it might be able to anyway. You really do have to be careful about what you post, where you post and who you allow access to your page on the internet.

I remember meeting Kimberly who was 15 years of age. She dropped out of high school in the 9th grade and could barely read. She loved social media and would spend countless hours on-line. Kimberly posted her picture on "kik" and began to communicate with a twenty four year old man who was definitely a "wolf" seeking meat. She met up with him a time or two and engaged into sexual encounters with him. It wasn't long before Kimberly became pregnant. He found out that she was pregnant and did not come around again. This was heartbreaking to hear, but this was truly a person who was a sexual predator on social media, seeking a vulnerable teenager. Always be cognizant of the things you post and who you meet on social media.

Remember, even if you hit delete, delete, delete, stuff in the cloud never dies!

Chapter 5

"For the wise man delights in establishing his merit, the brave man likes to show his courage in action, the covetous man is quick at seizing advantages, and the stupid man has no fear of death."
— Sun Tzu, The Art of War

CHAPTER 5

When I Know Better, I Do Better

How to fight the war and win

There are a lot of different ways you can win the war.

If you know you have the knowledge needed to fight the wars you face daily, you will find you have a much easier time in the fight. If one method doesn't work for one of the wars, don't be afraid to try something different. Be strategic in your battle. You can also read books, like the Bible, to find help.

The book of Ephesians 6:10-18 (New International Version) gives us directions on fighting and winning the war by putting on the full Armor of God.

[10]"Finally, be strong in the Lord and in his mighty power.[11] Put on the full armor of God, so that you can take your stand against the devil's schemes.[12] For our struggle is not against flesh and blood, but against the rulers, against the authorities, against the powers of this dark world and against the spiritual forces of evil in the heavenly realms.[13]

Therefore put on the full armor of God, so that when the day of evil comes, you may be able to stand your ground, and after you have done everything, to stand.[14] Stand firm then, with the belt of truth buckled around your waist, with the breastplate of righteousness in place,[15] and with your feet fitted with the readiness that comes from the gospel of peace.[16] In addition to all this, take up the shield of faith, with which you can extinguish all the flaming arrows of the evil one.[17] Take the helmet of salvation and the sword of the Spirit, which is the word of God.[18] And pray in the Spirit on all occasions with all kinds of prayers and requests. With this in mind, be alert and always keep on praying for all the Lord's people".

Get a mentor. Whether this is a spiritual mentor like a priest, a mental counselor, psychiatrist, a teacher, community leader or someone you look up to. Any of these kinds of people can help you with all aspects of the wars, though some may be better equipped for certain areas more than others are. But all will be able to help you in one way or another.

You can also try listening and watching motivational speeches and videos from leaders like myself, Les Brown and John Maxwell. We have all been where you are, and we have made these books and videos because we want to help you. There is often some sage advice you might find incredibly useful for your situation. Give it a try.

Another way to win the war is to find an activity through school or your community that you like and would want to participate in. This could be a sport or a craft, or volunteering at your local hospital or retirement home or school humanitarian group. You can even join a crafting or writing club, or a dance or cheer team. Regardless of what you join, you can find people who care about you and will want to help you. They will be the ones who will be a good influence on you, and are the kind of people you really want in your life. They can even introduce you to new and healthy ways to fight the daily wars you face.

There will also be people in your life who may try to negatively influence you. A big part of fighting and winning your daily wars is to get rid of these people. Get rid of the negative - do- nothing friends from your life because you are on a road to greatness and you do not want to carry that bogus, unproductive, envious, resentful, monopolizing, weightless, bottomless, contaminated luggage with you. Cutting these people out of your life is one of the best and hardest things you can do for yourself. People who get you to drink things that you should not be drinking, or who pressure you to use drugs or participate in illegal activities are people you should cut out of your life. You should reevaluate your relationship with people who constantly put you down, try to convince you that your choices or beliefs are wrong and try to cut you down or interfere with your happiness and progress. If you find these people are a part of your family, don't hesitate. Though it may be harder to do, it will be better for you in the long run. And if you can't do it right away, don't worry. Bit by bit works just as well.

Get ready to bury your old life and prepare to win the war against anger, anxiety, doubt, dishonesty, disobedience, fear, lust, sexual immorality, greed, envy and the lack of Faith in yourself. Remember, Preparing Girls for War allows you to enter into a new life with

The Father, Christ and the Spirit of Truth to be your Advocate, Comforter and Guide.

About the Author

 Dr. Erika Gibson is an energetic, high integrity Corporate Leader and Healthcare Provider who is known for her expertise as a Change Agent, Leadership Trainer, Speaker, Mentor, Process Improvement Consultant, Executive/Adolescent and Personal Coach. She has presented keynote speeches and workshops to Manage Care Organizations, the Restoring Hope Ministry (Georgia State Prison) and in many Churches across Georgia and Alabama. Erika Gibson received a Bachelor of Science (BS) Degree from Dillard University, a Master of Science Degree (MSA) from Central Michigan University, a Doctor of Medicine (MD) and Bachelor of Medicine/Bachelor of Surgery Degree (MBBS) from the University of Science Art and Technology School of Medicine and a Doctor of Chiropractic (DC) Degree from Life University. Amongst her educational degrees, Dr. Gibson is also certified as a Master Black Belt in Six Sigma Statistical Methodologies and a Certified Coach, Trainer, Speaker and Professional Mentor.

Erika began her career on a path that is rare among many other healthcare professionals. After many years of direct patient care, Dr. Erika transitioned into Executive Healthcare, where she gained extensive knowledge that allowed her the ability to impact policies, procedures and patient outcomes from an administrative outlook. Dr. Gibson has served in various leadership roles in Fortune 500 Companies as the Chief Operation Officer, Vice President, Southeast and Tristate General Manager, Executive Director, Clinical and Operational Director, Consultant and New Business Start-up Leader. She is the Co-Founder of Vitality Health Care, Incorporated.

Recognized for her expertise in cost savings, leadership, coaching, training, mentoring and public speaking, Dr. Gibson has provided leadership and consultation services to many Fortune 500 Companies in multispecialty Organizations. Erika has facilitated Member and Physician Advisory Groups and Clinical Advisory Panels for various Managed Care Organizations.

Dr. Erika Gibson has been married for 18 years and has two children. She is a member of Cascade United Methodist Church, The American College of Healthcare Executives, and Delta Sigma Theta Sorority, Incorporated.